Venerable Re...

The Story
of the Liberty Bell

Text by David Kimball

The author did no original research, and thus owes a particular debt to those upon whose research he relied: The many historians and curators from C. Richard Arena to Martin I. Yoelson, from Edward M. Riley to David C. G. Dutcher, who built the Independence National Historical Park's unique history note file; and John C. Paige, Historian with the National Park Service, Denver Service Center, whose "The Liberty Bell, A Special History Study" is definitive on the subject.

Many people suggested topics to be included, new ways to interpret old data, and gave other forms of assistance: Benjamin E. DeRoy, Philadelphia student of the Liberty Bell; Dr. Doris Fanelli, Curator and connoisseur of the Park's collection of Liberty Bell memorabilia; Curator Robert Giannini; Chief, Interpretive Support Services, Ron Thomson; and the Park's line Interpreters. Justin Kramer, whose CAST IN AMERICA contains an excellent discussion of 18th Century casting methods, graciously permitted use of illustrations from his book.

Of course, the author would owe no one had not Eastern National Park and Monument Association funded this publication, and had not the Park's Division of Interpretation and Visitor Services, under Chief Kathy Dilonardo, selected him to write it. He commends this choice, and thanks the entire Division for their assistance in preparing the text and the thoroughness of their review of it. Any errors in fact, interpretation or style which may remain prove only that the author can make more errors than any group can find and correct.

— David Kimball

©1989 Eastern National Park & Monument Association
Philadelphia, PA
Printed in USA
ISBN # 0-915992-43-4

Contents

BY order of the Assembly of the Province of Pensylvania

BY ORDER OF THE ASSEMBLY OF THE PROVINCE OF PENSYLVANIA

for the State house in the City of Philad^{a} 1752

FOR THE STATE HOUSE IN PHILAD^{A}

Proclaim Liberty thro' all the Land

PROCLAIM LIBERTY THROUGHOUT ALL THE LAND

to all the Inhabitants thereof Levit.XXV. 10.

UNTO ALL THE INHABITANTS THEREOF LEV. XXV X.

Comparison of the
inscription on the Liberty Bell,
with the inscription ordered by
Isaac Norris in 1751.

"And ye shall hallow the fiftieth year,
and proclaim liberty throughout all the land
unto all the inhabitants thereof:
it shall be a jubilee unto you;
and ye shall return every man unto his possession
and ye shall return every man unto his family."

Holy Bible,
King James version,
Leviticus,
chapter 25, verse 10

LEV. XXV v X. PROCLAIM

IN PHILAD^A. BY ORDER

PASS AND STOW

PHILAD^A

MDCCL

Introduction

The Liberty Bell is not only our nation's most famous and most venerated object, it has become a world-wide symbol of freedom. Each year it attracts hundreds of thousands of visitors.

As befits such a famous object, much is known about the bell's origins. We know why it was made, who made it, how much it weighed, how much it cost, and when it was finally hoisted up and hung in the steeple of Pennsylvania's State House (Independence Hall). After 1852, when, cracked and useless it was taken down from the steeple and put on display in the Assembly Room of the Hall, we know its every famous visitor, its every move.

But strangely, for the ninety-nine years between 1753 when it was raised to the State House steeple, and 1852 when it was lowered again, we know relatively little about it. During those years, it rang in anonymity. It was simply one of several bells in the city. The historical record seldom tells us when the bell rang and no contemporary that we know of bothered to note when the now famous crack first occurred.

Ironically, it was during those years of obscurity that a quiet yet significant transformation took place. Gradually, this State House bell of debatable quality evolved into an enduring symbol of freedom. Slowly it became a national and ultimately an international memorial to liberty. This is the story of that transformation.

Part One

The Early Years

Warner
Dubrey
Dubrey
Peel
Jones
Meredith
Fair mount
Sculls Ferry
Spangeles Ferry
Turner
Ferry
Gardner
P. Jones
Mill
White
Lower Ferry
Jones
Jones
White
Gray
Gray
Hins
J. Pemberton
Polb
PASSY
Crouse
Duchee
Rambo
Cadwaladr
Morris
Lorens
Hannis
Cox
Cox
Griffith
Penrose
Hannis
River
UNK

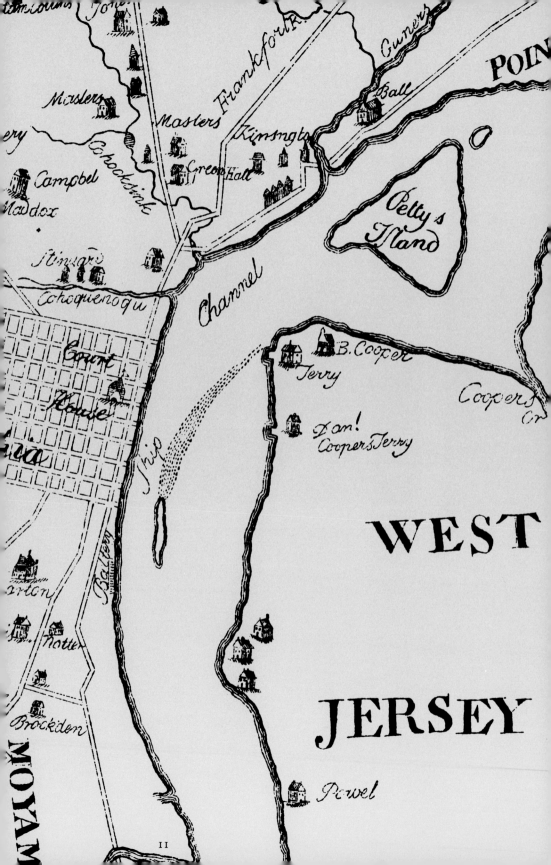

William Penn

Penn's Province — Something Special

In 1681, King Charles of England gave William Penn title to almost all of what is now Pennsylvania. At the same time, the King gave Penn *"free, full, and absolute power...to ordayne, make, enact and...publish any Laws whatsoever"* within the land grant's 45,000 square miles.

Penn, a religious and political reformer, seized this opportunity to put his ideas into action. In 1682, he exercised the power given to him by the King and issued a charter of government for his new domain. To all who believed in God, Penn granted freedom of conscience. All Christian white adult males who paid taxes could vote. The colonists could make their own laws through an elected legislature.

Penn's charter created a two-house legislature. The people elected the lower house, the Assembly. The Governor (Penn or someone he appointed), together with the upper house, the Council, proposed all legislation, executed the laws, and appointed judges. The Assembly could only veto or amend legislation proposed by the Council, and could meet only when called into session by the Governor.

While most of the early settlers to Pennsylvania were Quakers or German pietists, they were a contentious and, at least to Penn, an ungrateful lot. Some of the most contentious and least grateful even got elected to the Assembly, which soon extorted for itself the power to initiate all legislation and decide for itself when it would meet. By 1701, Penn recognized the Assembly's newly won power by granting another charter, the Charter of Privileges. In less than two decades, the Pennsylvania Assembly had become the most powerful and independent colonial legislature in America.

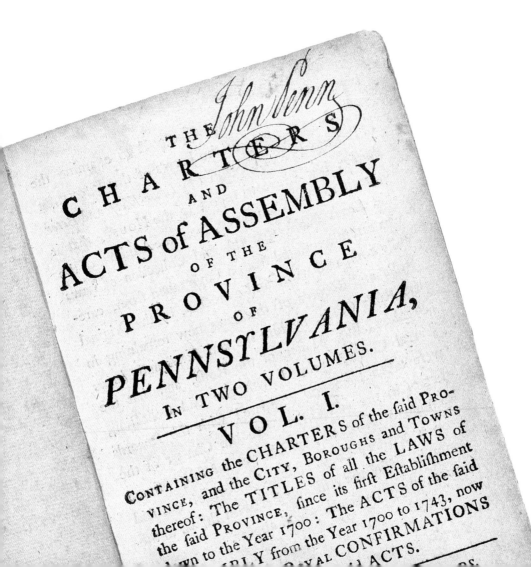

THE CHARTERS AND ACTS of ASSEMBLY OF THE PROVINCE OF PENNSYLVANIA, IN TWO VOLUMES.

VOL. I.

CONTAINING the CHARTERS of the said Province, and the CITY, BOROUGHS and TOWNS thereof: The TITLES of all the LAWS of the said PROVINCE, since its first Establishment down to the Year 1700: The ACTS of the said ASSEMBLY from the Year 1700 to 1743, now ROYAL CONFIRMATIONS

A Home for the Legislature, and a Bell

For twenty-eight years after winning the Charter of Privileges, this most powerful of colonial legislatures met in taverns or private homes. A suitable state house, owned and controlled by the Assembly, was badly needed. But they had little money, and Pennsylvanians hated paying taxes.

Finally, in 1729, Assembly Speaker Andrew Hamilton came up with an idea. He proposed printing paper money, loaning it to deserving Pennsylvanians, and using the interest on these loans to pay for government expenses, including construction of a state house.

Andrew Hamilton

Appropriately, when the Assembly approved Hamilton's plan, they also chose him as chairman of a board of trustees charged with selecting a site for, designing, and overseeing construction of the state house. Hamilton dominated the board and the process. The result, the Pennsylvania State House, became colonial America's most imposing public building.

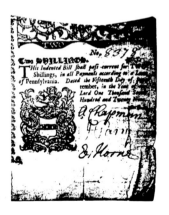

Even so, the Assembly was not completely satisfied. In November of 1749, they *"Ordered, That the Superintendents of the State-House, proceed, ... to carry up a Building on the South-side of the said House to contain the Staircase, with a suitable Place thereon for hanging a Bell."* Not until October 15, 1751, nearly two years after ordering a steeple built, did the Assembly finally take steps to purchase the bell.

A MAP OF PHILADELPHᴵ

With a PERSPECTIVE VIEW of the STAᵀ

This Building stands in a Square of 396 Feet
by 255 Surrounded by a high Wall. the Ground
is to be laid out in walks with Rows of Trees
In the Body of the Building are two Rooms of
40 Feet Square & 20 Feet high one for the Assem
bly the other for the supreme Court between
which is an Entry of 40 Feet by 20 on the
Second Floor is the Councils Chamber and Com
mette Room with a Gallery 13 Feet by 20
The Publick Offices are kept in the Wings
it was founded Anno 1732.——

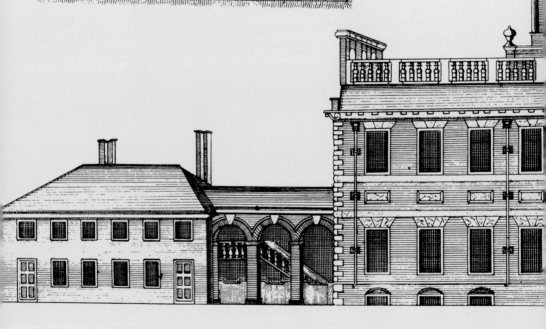

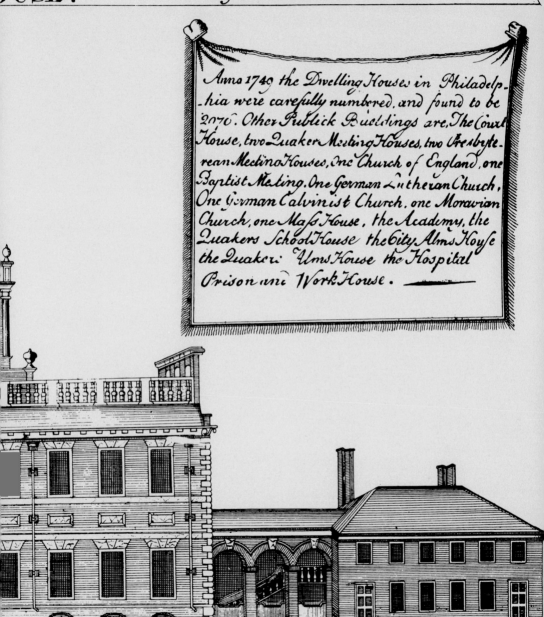

Anno 1749 the Dwelling Houses in Philadelp-
hia were carefully numbered, and found to be
2076. Other Publick Buildings are, The Court
House, two Quaker Meeting Houses, two Presbyte-
rean Meeting Houses, One Church of England, one
Baptist Meting, One German Lutheran Church,
One German Calvinist Church, one Moravian
Church, one Mass House, the Academy, the
Quakers School House the City Alms House
the Quakers Alms House the Hospital
Prison and Work House. ———

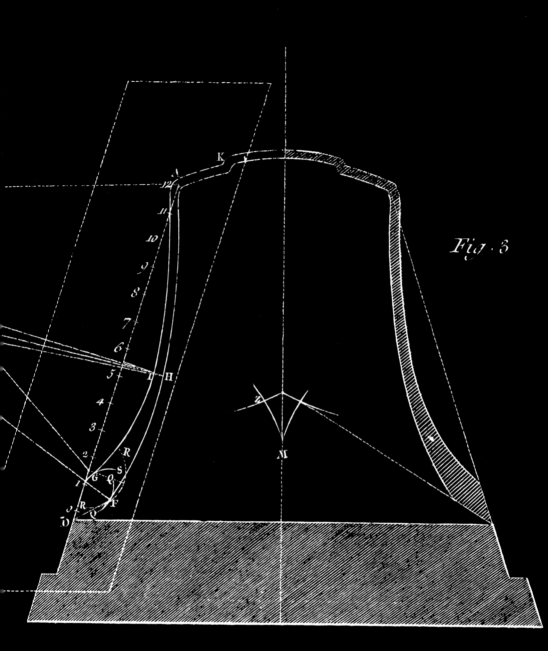

Fig. 3

The Third Time is the Charm — Getting a State House Bell

It was Assembly Speaker and Chairman of the State House Superintendents, Isaac Norris, who wrote the Assembly's London agent, Robert Charles, asking him to procure a *"good Bell of about two thousand pounds weight."* Norris' letter, of which we have only a clerk's copy, went on:

"Let the Bell be cast by the best Workmen & examined carefully before it is Shipped with the following words well shaped in large letters round it vizt. /By order of the Assembly of the Povince [sic] of Pensylvania for the State house in the City of Philada 1752// //and Underneath // Proclaim Liberty thro' all the Land to all the Inhabitants thereof. - Levit. XXV. 10"

Years after Norris chose this inscription, a local historian checked the cited verse, noticed that it also said, "And ye shall hallow the fiftieth year," and decided that the inscription was chosen to honor the 1701 Charter of Privileges. This made some sense since the liberties provided by the Charter were certainly extensive enough to prompt Norris to commemorate them on this new bell. But Norris' ancestors had helped extort the Charter from William Penn. Norris was himself an anti-proprietary leader. If he, in fact, intended to specifically commemorate the 50th anniversary of the 1701 Charter, why did he specify 1752, not 1751, for the bell's inscription? Since Norris himself never mentioned commemoration or any other explanation for the inscription, perhaps historians have spent too much time reading

Bell Diagram,
DIDEROT ENCYCLOPEDIA

between the lines? The fact does remain that Pennsylvanians were justifiably proud of the freedoms
they enjoyed, and were not shy about celebrating and
protecting them.

If the inscription did honor the Charter, the Penns
were not particularly grateful. Thomas Penn,
William's son, wrote in 1757 that the Assembly
*"...tho they pretend no exception can be taken to
their having misapplied Money, I think their Hospital,
Steeple, Bells, unecessary Library, with several
other things are reasons why they should not have the
appropriations to themselves...."*

Whatever the underlying reason for the inscription,
agent Charles, as directed, ordered the bell
from Thomas Lester of Whitechapel Foundry.
We let the record tell what happened thereafter.

*"1752 May To cash for the cost
of a Bell wth frt [freight]
& Insurance £ 150.13.8."*
(Robert Charles's bill to the Province)

August 9, 1752
"We are looking for our Bell daily."
(Isaac Norris to R. Charles)

September 1, 1752
*"The Bell is come ashore & in good order...
'tho we have not yet tryd the sound   we are making
a Clock for it."*
(Norris to Charles)

In that Letter I gave Information *that our Bell* was generally liked & app^{vd} of but in a few days after my writing I had the Mortification to hear that it was cracked by a stroke of the clapper without any other violence as it was hung up to try the sound the this was not very agreable to us we concluded to send it back by Cap^{tn} Budden but he could not take it on board upon which two Ingenious Work-Men undertook to cast it here & I am just now Informed they have this Day opened the mould I have got a good Bell which I confess pleases me very much that we should first Venture upon and sussed in the greatest Bell cast for ought I know in English America the mould was finished in a very Masterly manner & the Letters I am told are better than in our $_{\wedge}^{old one}$ when we broke up the Metal our Judges here generally aggreed it was too high & brittle & cast several little bells out of it to try the sound & strength & fixed upon a mixture of an ounce andahalf of copper to a pound of the old Bell & in this proportion we now have it

The House at their last sitting

March 10, 1753

"*I gave Information that our Bell was generally liked &
appvd of but in a few days after my writing I had the
Mortification to hear that it was cracked by a stroke of the
clapper without any other viollence as it was hung up to
try the sound...two Ingenious Work-Men undertook to cast
it here & I am just now Informed that they have this day
opened the mould & have got a good Bell...when we broke
up the metal [of the Whitechapel bell] our Judges hare
generally aggreed it was too high and brittle...& fixed upon
a mixture of an ounce and a half of copper to a pound of
the old Bell & in this proportion we now have it.*"
(Norris to Charles)

How Bells Were Made In The 1750s

Eighteenth Century bell casting began with designing the bell, a process governed by mathematical formulas developed over the centuries.

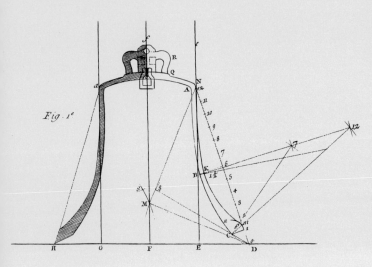

Fig. 1ᵉ

The diagrams below courtesy of Justin Kramer, CAST IN AMERICA.

Constructing a Bell Mold

Once the design was finished, workmen dug a hole deep enough that ground level would be six inches higher than the top of the finished bell and wide enough to provide working room around the completed bell. They then built a hollow brick oven in the shape of, but slightly smaller than, the inside of the bell, and open at the top.

Next, a profile of the inside of the bell was cut from a board and this template was mounted on a pole standing in the center of the oven, resulting in sort of an oversized draftsman's compass. Then, layers of clay or loam mixed with horse manure, horse hair and hemp to increase cohesion were added to the brick oven, shaped with the template and dried until this inner mold, or core, was complete. Drying was speeded by putting burning coals in the oven.

The core was then lubricated with ashes or pig fat, a template of the outside of the bell cut, and a model of the bell built from the same material and by the same process used to form the core.

The clay "bell" was then lubricated, and an outside mold, or cope, built up. When the cope was sufficiently thick, it was very carefully lifted clear of the core, and the clay bell was broken up and removed.

1. Bell profile transferred to strickle board

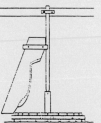

2. Beginning of brick sub-core.

3. Bearing board installed.

Bell Casting, ENCYCLOPEDIA DIDEROT

Some foundries, including Pass and Stow, would have cast the inscriptions and decorative rings in wax, and attached them to the model bell, so their copes would already have the incriptions when lifted off the core. Other foundries, including Whitechapel, cut a strip out of the inside of the cope, and replaced it with fine soft clay in which they impressed the inscription.

However the inscription was formed, casting could now begin. The cope was carefully lowered over the core. A separate mold of the cannon (the loops used to attach the bell to its yoke) was lowered into place, the pit was filled with sand to keep the cope from shifting, and the molten bell metal poured into the space between core and cope.

4. Loam Core.

5. False bell
with wax letters.

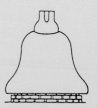

6. Complete mold.

March 29, 1753
"Ed. Woolley this day has
begun to raise the Belfry in order to hang the Bell."
(Charles Norris to James Wright)

April 14, 1753
"A native of the Isle of Malta and a son of Charles Stow
were the persons who undertook to cast our Bell...but upon
tryal it seems they have added too much copper...but they
were so teized with the witicisms of the Town that they...will
be very soon ready to make a second essay."
(Norris to Charles)

June 11, 1753
"Last Week was raised and fix'd in the
Statehouse Steeple, the new great Bell, cast here
by Pass and Stow, weighing 2080 lbs."
(NEW YORK MERCURY)

July 3, 1753
"July 3 For Recasting the State house bell
wt 2044
at 4 pence Sterling pr. lb.
                    £ 34.1.4
For 37 lbs. additional wt at 14 pence per lb.
Sterling   2.3.2
                    _____

                    £ 36.4.6
(Pass and Stow's bill)

November 8, 1753

"We got our Bell new cast here and it has been used some
time but tho' some are of opinion it will do I Own I
do not like it   if therefore Lester will cast us up another...
[at] two pence a pound...I will engage to return the Metal
of our present Bell by the first oppo."
(Norris to Charles)

March 1, 1754

"To cash for the cost of a Bell
then sent for Service £ 137.2.6."
(Robert Charles's bill)

May 3, 1754

"...we have not yet concluded, whether to send back
our old bell and pay for the casting or keep them both."
(Norris to Charles)

May 1754

"Resolved, that the said
Superintendents [of the State House] do pay for the
new Bell, and keep the Old One for such Uses as this
House may hereafter appoint."
(Votes of Assembly)

So, after two years of effort and three castings on
two continents, the Pennsylvania Assembly appeared
now to have two bells, one of questionable quality.

Part Two

Years of Obscurity

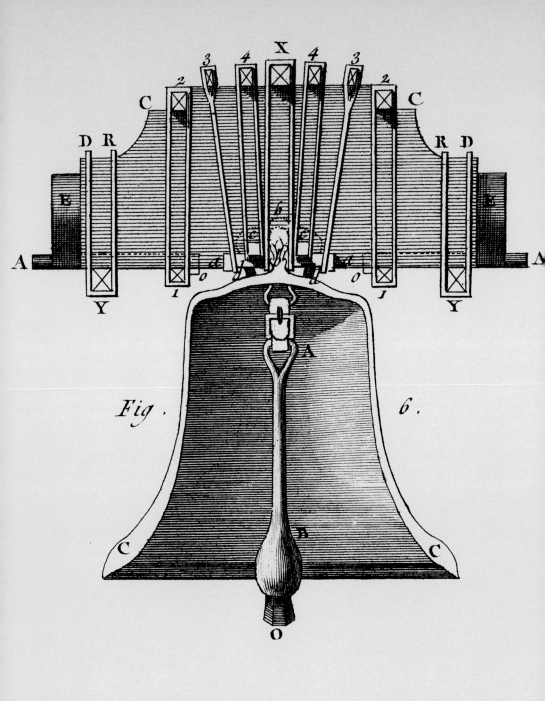

Fig. 6.

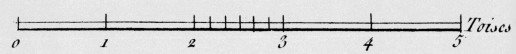

Toises

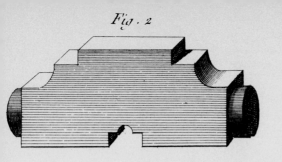

Fig. 2.

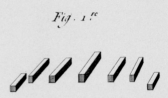

Fig. 1.ʳᵉ

Fig. 3.

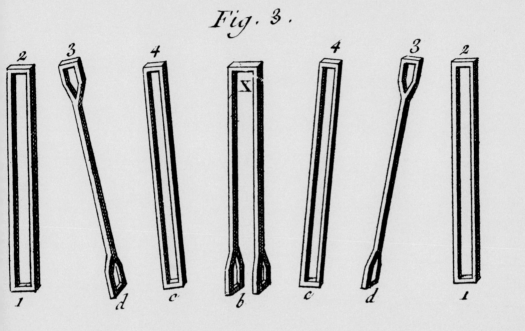

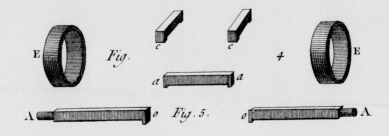

Fig. 4

Fig. 5.

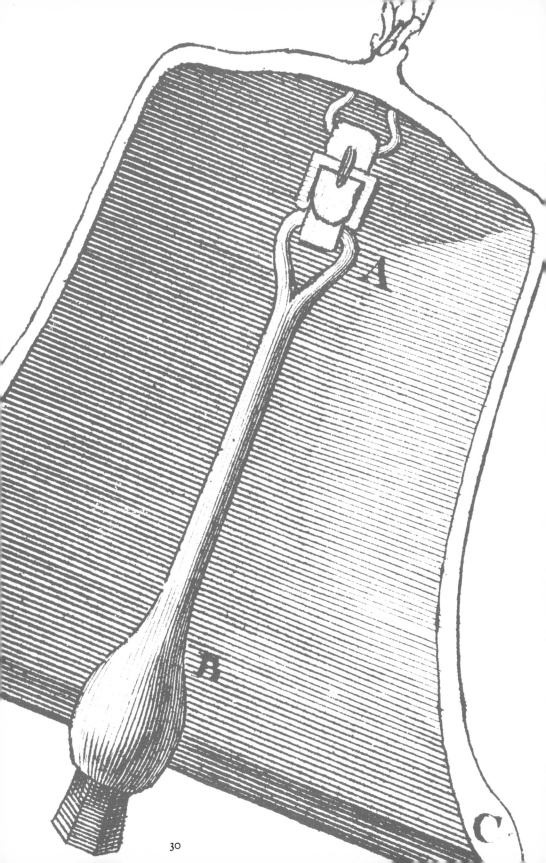

When this second Whitechapel bell arrived, it sounded no better to Philadelphia ears than Pass and Stow's bell. So, the American bell with its prophetic *"Proclaim Liberty"* inscription stayed in the State House steeple. The new English bell was hoisted into a cupola on the State House roof and attached to the State House clocks. There it dutifully struck the hours.

From its lofty place in the steeple, it was the Pass and Stow bell that called the Assembly to its meetings. Thus, it rang to announce the Assembly meeting of February 3, 1757, the session that voted to send Benjamin Franklin to England to look after the colony's interests. In the 1760s it summoned sessions to debate the Sugar Act, Stamp Act, Townshend Act and other acts of Parliament which ultimately triggered the American Revolution.

It probably also rang, with the other bells of the city, on various civic occasions -the death of King George II and the accession of King George III, as well as the various public meetings which greeted Britain's attempts to tighten control over the colonies.

While we know that the city bells rang dozens of times in the years before the Revolution, only three times was the State House bell specifically mentioned. In the early 1760s, the Assembly permitted St. Paul's Church to use the bell to announce worship until their church building was completed and a bell installed. On October 5, 1765,

John Hughes, the Stamp agent for Philadelphia, noted that *"the state-house bell muffled"* rang to summon Philadelphians to a public meeting to discuss the Stamp Act. He noted the occasion because of the very personal message that resulted from the meeting. *"... [I]f I did not immediately resign my office,"* Hughes wrote, *"my house should be pulled down and my substance destroyed."* Finally, in 1772 people living near the State House petitioned the Assembly *"that they are much incommoded and distressed by the too frequent Ringing of the great Bell in the Steeple."*

July 8, 1776 -Did the Bell Proclaim Liberty?

Relief for these petitioners was on the way. Earlier, the Assembly had decided it did not like the State House steeple's appearance, and would spend no money on needed repairs. On October 19, 1774, they actually *"took into Consideration the ruinous Condition of the State-House Steeple, and... Ordered, ... the wooden Part of the Steeple taken down, and the Brick Work cheaply covered."* Although the Revolution intervened and the steeple was not torn down immediately, its condition was so bad that it may have kept the State House bell from announcing the great events of 1774 and 1775 -the First Continental Congress, news of Lexington and Concord, the Second Continental Congress, and Washington's departure from Philadelphia to take command of the Continental Army.

Reading of the Declaration,
Copyright Louis Glanzman

Did the bell ring on July 4, 1776? No it did not. In fact, no city bells rang on July 4th. Since Congress met in closed session, the public knew little about either Richard Henry Lee's resolution calling for independence or Thomas Jefferson's draft declaration.

Declaring independence was, however, a momentous step deserving of wide publicity and, right after Congress approved the Declaration on July 4, it ordered the document printed and sent *"to the several assemblies... or councils of safety, and to the several commanding officers of the continental troops; that it be proclaimed in each of the United States, and at the head of the Army."*

The Declaration appeared in newspapers as early as July 6, but most people did not read newspapers. So Philadelphia's Committee of Safety ordered the document read in the yard behind the State House at noon on July 8 (perhaps the first public reading of the document). It was on the 8th that the city's bells rang throughout the day and into the night. Unless the State House steeple was so rotten that a swinging bell might topple it, we assume that, on at least this one occasion, the State House bell joined in the revolutionary celebration.

How The Bell Was Most Probably Rung

Ringing a Bell

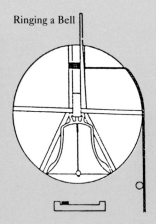

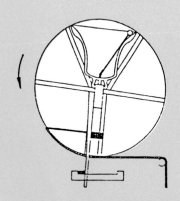

We think the Liberty Bell was mounted on a frame and rung by means of a wheel, as shown in the accompanying illustrations.

1. Bell in down position.

2. Bell set at "hand stroke" (arrow indicates direction bell will rotate when rope is pulled).

Diagrams courtesy of Justin Kramer, CAST IN AMERICA.

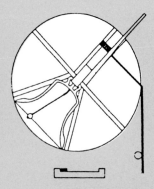

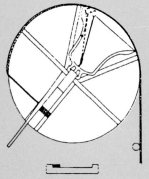

3. Bell rotates: rope begins to wind on wheel.

4. Clapper strikes bell and rebounds.

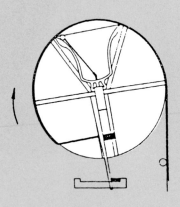

5. Stay moves slider towards stop.

6. Slider reaches stop, bell is set at "back stroke" (arrow indicates direction bell will rotate when rope is pulled).

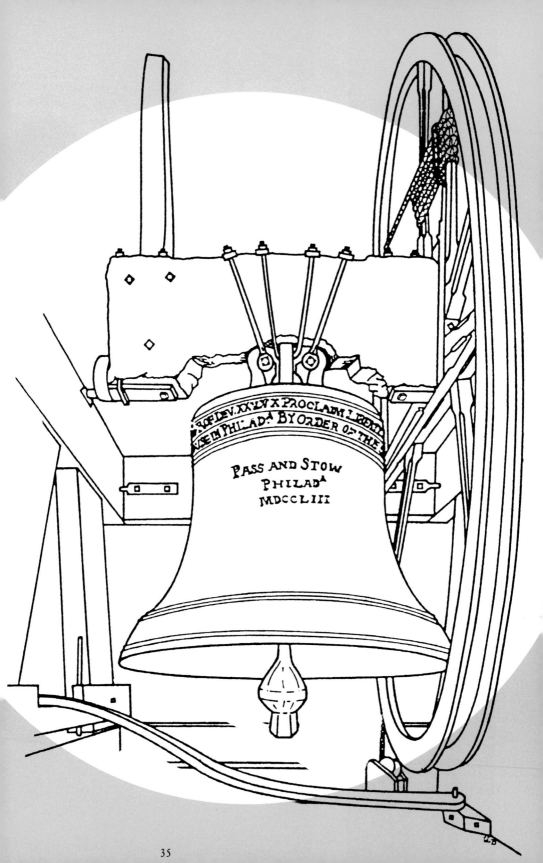

Off to Allentown

In 1777, the city bells did ring on July 4 to celebrate the nation's birthday. But the war was not going well. By early September, General Howe's British army threatened Philadelphia and the city prepared to remove anything of value to the enemy. Since bells could be melted and, with the addition of a little copper, recast into brass cannon, all the city's bells were taken down and shipped inland. A contemporary diarist recorded that, on September 23, the wagon carrying the State House bell broke down near Bethlehem, Pennsylvania. Another wagon was found and, according to long-standing and uncontroverted tradition, the bell went on to Allentown and storage in the basement of Zion Reformed Church.

The Steeple Removed

The British evacuated Philadelphia in June 1778, and the city's bells returned. With the State House steeple in worse shape than ever, the State House bell seems to have been stored, probably in one of the munitions sheds which stood on either side of the State House.

Artist's conception of how the bell might have been moved. Courtesy, Liberty Bell Shrine Allentown, PA.

Gradually, preparations were made to return the bell to some degree of usefulness. First, in 1781, the rotted steeple was torn down. Then a temporary roof was built over the brick tower and the State House bell hoisted up to the upper floors, but probably not yet re-hung. Not until 1785, when a new bell frame was built and three of the tower windows were replaced with sounding boards, was the bell finally back in service.

While this new enclosed location must have reduced the bell's effectiveness, it continued to call the state legislature into session, to summon the voters to hand in their ballots at the State House windows, and to celebrate Washington's birthday and the Fourth of July. For a while in 1789 and later, it called students of the University of Pennsylvania to their classes in neighboring Philosophical Hall.

In 1799, the state capital moved to Lancaster, leaving the State House vacant except for court sessions. The bell, however, continued to call voters to the State House, to celebrate national patriotic holidays, and to mark such occasions as the deaths of famous Americans or the arrival in the city of distinguished visitors.

New Steeple, New Bell

In 1816, Pennsylvania decided to sub-divide the State House yard and sell it as building lots. At the same time, the county of Philadelphia "modern-ized" the room used by Congress when they met in the State House. Shocked by these changes, the city of Philadelphia promptly bought the State House and its yard for $70,000.

Cross section of the tower and steeple of Independence Hall.

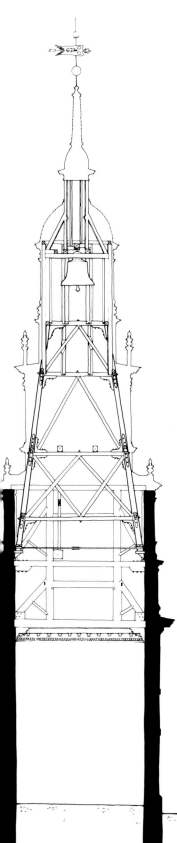

As soon as it received title to the State House, the city considered repairs. In 1821, Philadelphia City Councils (there were two councils at the time), bought a new bell for the clocks on the ends of the State House, and in 1828, they decided to reconstruct the building's wooden steeple and, almost by chance, initiated the country's first historic preservation movement.

Reconstructing even a portion of a building was a novel idea. There were no historical architects to prepare restoration plans. Nobody had undertaken any restorations so there was no experience to learn from. The plan that evolved called for replacing the old and unreliable State House clock with a new one in the new steeple. The new clock deserved, and would receive, a new larger bell.

A local foundry owner, John Wilbank, proposed to cast a 4,000 pound bell for 45 cents a pound, and to pay $400 for the old clock bell. When the Wilbank bell was hoisted up to the new steeple in December 1828, it promptly became *"the State House bell."* The old State House bell, the Pass and Stow bell, remained in the fourth floor of the brick part of the State House tower.

Sixty years later, Wilbank's son claimed that his father never got the old clock bell, even though $400 was deducted from the price of the new bell. The family erroneously claimed the Pass and Stow bell. Since the 1821 clock bell disappeared without a word, Wilbank probably did take it. But even if he did not, the Pass and Stow bell was never part of the bargain.

Part Three

The Crack

Metallic Content

Bell Casting, ENCYCLOPEDIA DIDEROT

In 1960, *The Franklin Institute took drillings weighing five to ten milligrams from either side of the crack in the Liberty Bell. The International Nickel Company analyzed the content of these drillings. In 1975, scientists from Winterthur Museum and the DuPont Company used an X-Ray Florescence Analyzer to determine the metallic content at ten points around the rim. These readings vary to a great degree. The table to the right gives the* ranges found in the twelve areas sampled in the two studies. A precise determination could be made only by melting the bell, thoroughly mixing the molten metal, and then taking a sample for analysis. This seems undesirable.

Element Liberty Bell Percent (range)	
Copper	Silver
64.95 - 73.10	0.14 - 0.26
Tin	Antimony
24.00 - 30.16	0.08 - 0.18
Lead	Arsenic
1.30 - 5.47	0.19 - 0.42
Zinc	Gold
0.25 - 1.65	0.02 - 0.06
Iron	Nickel
0.00 - 0.87	0.00 - 0.28

Above, a worker pushes the last of metal through to the tap-hole trough.

While the Pass and Stow bell might have become a venerated national symbol had it not cracked, it is precisely that crack that now distinguishes it. Inevitably, a history of the bell must address the question, *"When did the bell crack?"*

Unfortunately, a precise answer is elusive. All that can be said with certainty is that the crack occurred sometime between 1817 and 1846. Here are the facts, and the legends, about the crack:

One

On March 5, 1824, a Philadelphia newspaper published a poem about the old State House bell. On September 3, another local paper ran a story about the bell, and quoted its inscription. Neither mentioned any crack.

Two

Between February 7 and December 27, 1828, Philadelphia City Councils occasionally discussed the new bell, clock and steeple. None of these discussions indicates that the old bell was unusable.

Three

In 1829, both the SATURDAY EVENING POST and THE CASKET described the State House. *"In the attic story of the basement of the steeple [the brick part] is suspended the great bell."* Both quote the inscription; neither mentions a crack.

Four

On June 30, 1831, City Councils agreed to let the young men of the city ring *"the old State House bell"* on the Fourth of July.

Five

In 1837, a guidebook mentioned that the old State House bell was not in use, but didn't mention any crack. In the same year, a stylized rendering of the bell appeared in an anti-slavery publication showing the bell uncracked.

Six

In 1841, a British traveler reported that *"This bell, though no longer used for general purposes, still occupies the place in which it was originally hung, and...is used only on very special occasions, such as the anniversary of the Declaration of Independence, the visit of any distinguished personage..."* On April 7, according to local reporters, the *"old bell"* was tolled upon the death of President William Henry Harrison, the first President to die in office.

Seven

The February 29, 1844, PUBLIC LEDGER carried a story on the bell, but did not mention any crack.

Eight

The February 1846 PUBLIC LEDGER reported, under the heading *"The old Independence Bell," "This venerable relic of the Revolution rang its last clear note on Monday last [February 23],...and now hangs in the great city steeple irreparably cracked and forever dumb. It had been cracked long before, but was put in order for that day [Washington's birthday] by having the edges of the fracture filed...It gave out clear notes and loud, and appeared to be in excellent condition until noon, when it received a sort of compound fracture in a zig-zag direction through one of its sides...."*

Nine

In 1848, the PUBLIC LEDGER mentioned in passing that the bell had cracked in the autumn of 1845.

Ten

On March 9, 1876, the volunteer curator of Independence Hall, Col. Frank Etting, announced that he had found out that the bell had cracked in 1835, while tolling during the funeral procession for Chief Justice John Marshall. This claim was never documented, although widely accepted.

Eleven

Around 1884, John Wilbank's son claimed the bell had cracked in 1824 while welcoming Lafayette to Philadelphia.

Dimensions Of The Liberty Bell

Circumference at lip	*12 feet*
Circumference at crown	*6 feet 11 1/4 inches*
Lip to the crown	*3 feet*
Height over the crown	*2 feet 3 inches*
Thickness at lip	*3 inches*
Thickness at crown	*1 1/4 inches*
Weight	*2080 pounds**
Length of clapper	*3 feet 2 inches*
Weight of clapper	*44 1/2 pounds*
Cost	*unknown***
Weight of yoke	*200 pounds*
Yoke's wood	*American Elm*

Diagram shows section of the internal relief suspension of the Liberty Bell.

*   *Less any amount chipped off the lip or drilled out of the crack. To our knowledge, the Liberty Bell has never been weighed.*

**   *The true cost of the Liberty Bell is the charge made by Whitechapel, including freight and insurance (150 pounds, 13 shillings, 8 pence Sterling), less any credit given on the second Whitechapel bell (unknown), plus whatever Pass and Stow charged for their two bells. We know Pass and Stow charged 36 pounds, 4 shillings, 6 pence Sterling for one casting, but we are not certain that this was their only charge.*

Twelve

In 1899, Philadelphian John Sartain claimed the bell had cracked while celebrating passage by Parliament of the Catholic Emancipation Act of 1828.

Thirteen

In June of 1903, a letter to the editor of the PUBLIC LEDGER claimed that the Journals of Philadelphia City Councils proved that the bell cracked welcoming Lafayette in 1824. (They do not.)

Fourteen

In 1911, Joseph Rauch wrote the NEW YORK TIMES that, as a boy, he had helped ring the bell on Washington's birthday by pulling a rope attached to the clapper, and this was when the bell cracked.

From this evidence, all we can be sure of is that the famous and familiar wide crack dates from February 1846. It is the result of an attempt to fix an earlier crack by stop-drilling, a process of drilling and filing. We also know that the bell could not be rung after February 23rd of that year, when the repair failed and the crack lengthened.

We do not know when the crack which was filed out in 1846 occurred. Our best guess is that it occurred between 1841 and 1845, as the bell celebrated Washington's birthday or July 4th. Unless a reliable newspaper story, diary entry, or letter mentioning the cracking of the bell turns up, we can be no more precise than that.

Part Four

Fame

Shown an uncaptioned photo of the Liberty Bell, most Americans could identify it. Shown an uncaptioned photograph of the inkstand used to sign the Declaration of Independence and the Constitution, or the chair from which Washington presided over the Constitutional Convention, most Americans would be baffled. Why and how the Liberty Bell became accepted as a national symbol is a fascinating tale of legend occasionally reinforced with fact.

S O N N E T

SUGGESTED BY THE INSCRIPTION ON THE
PHILADELPHIA LIBERTY BELL.

It is no tocsin of affright we sound,
    Summoning nations to the conflict dire ;-
    No fearful peal from cities wrapped in fire
Echoes, at our behest, the land around :-
Yet would we rouse our country's utmost bound

Early Local Interest

The evolution of the State House bell into the Liberty Bell can be traced to 1824. On September 3 of that year, a Philadelphia newspaper ran a story quoting the bell's inscription, noting that the bell had been the first to announce the Declaration of Independence, that it rang to call voters to the polls, and that it would ring to welcome Lafayette back to Philadelphia. In May 1829, the SATURDAY EVENING POST also quoted what it referred to as the bell's *"prophetic inscription."* As early as 1831, City Councils regarded permission to ring the bell as a special privilege. Throughout the 1820s and 30s, the number of visitors making the pilgrimage up the tower steps to see the bell gradually increased. By 1837, a local guidebook included a reference to the bell making it a bona fide, although still a minor, tourist attraction. The bell, according to the guidebook, had been used to call people together to hear independence proclaimed and was *"still preserved in the steeple of the building, as a relic of the heroic age of American history."*

Abolitionists Name the Liberty Bell

Early representation of the Liberty Bell. From the anti-slavery booklet, THE LIBERTY BELL, published by the Massachusetts Anti-Slavery Fair, Boston, 1839.

The bell was first introduced to a national audience as a symbol of the abolitionist movement. An 1837 edition of LIBERTY, published by the New York Anti-Slavery Society, used a stylized but recognizable State House bell as a frontispiece. This version emphasized the words *"Proclaim Liberty"* and *"to ALL the Inhabitants."* In 1839, a Boston abolitionist group published a pamphlet containing a poem about the bell titled *"The Liberty Bell."* The poem was reprinted in the national abolitionist publication, THE LIBERATOR, in November 1839, and the *"Liberty Bell"* soon became nationally known.

Ring, Grandfather! Ring!

But the Liberty Bell did not become identified exclusively, or even primarily, with the abolitionists. Nobody did more to popularize the bell than a now forgotten American writer, George Lippard.

On January 2, 1847, one of a series of legends about the American Revolution by Lippard, *"Fourth of July, 1776"* appeared in the SATURDAY COURIER magazine. In it, Lippard told the tale of an aged bellman waiting in the State House steeple for a signal to ring the State House bell as soon as Congress agreed to declare independence. As he waited, he began to doubt that Congress had the courage to break away from Great Britain. At the most dramatic moment, the bellman's blue-eyed tow-headed grandson, who had been listening at the door of Congress, appeared in the courtyard shouting *"Ring, Grandfather! Ring!"*

This fictional account, far more dramatic than the facts, caught the nation's fancy. Frequently reprinted, it helped link the Liberty Bell to the Declaration of Independence in the public mind.

GRAHAM'S MAGAZINE.

VOL. XLIV.   PHILADELPHIA, JUNE, 1854.   No. 6.

The Bellman informed of the passage of the Declaration of Independence. (See page 582.)

"*The Bellman informed of the passage of the Declaration of Independence.*"
Lippard's legend of the Liberty Bell was incorporated by Joel Tyler Headley in his LIFE OF GEORGE WASHINGTON, which ran serially in GRAHAM'S MAGAZINE, June 1854.

The Liberty Bell becomes an Icon

In 1850, historian Benson Lossing included a sketch of the Liberty Bell in his PICTORIAL FIELD BOOK OF THE AMERICAN REVOLUTION, and included Lippard's story as historical fact. In 1853, President Franklin Pierce visited Philadelphia, saw the bell, and spoke of it as representing the American Revolution and American liberty.

Its fame continued to grow as it appeared in guide-books, and as Lippard's story was repeated by other writers. In the 1860s, the bell appeared on souvenir plates and during the centennial of American Independence in 1876, the bell appeared on a host of souvenir items -the highest accolade the American people can bestow. It inspired numer-ous poems, a Sousa march, and an opera. Innumerable replicas ranging in scale from the tiny to the gigantic have been made. The bell has appeared on six United States postage stamps, on two coins, and on food coupons. It has appeared in the name or logo of companies from distilleries to life insurance companies, and many political groups have used its likeness in their campaigns. An obvious play upon its name, the title *"Liberty Belles"* has been used by woman's political groups, beauty contests, and pornographic movies.

However, the surest indication of the Liberty Bell's enduring place in the Nation's conscience is the tendency to turn to it on occasions of joy or sorrow. Whether to lay a commemorative wreath, protest government's actions or inactions, or simply gain reassurance in times of trouble, people turn to the bell. As the 19th century progressed, that became easier to do.

Liberty Bell displayed on
various United States stamps
and memorabilia.

LIBERTY BELL ®

PHILADELPHIA

The City of Brotherly Love

The Liberty Bell, between 1854
and 1876, stood on display in
the Assembly Room on a thirteen-
sided pedestal representing the
thirteen original states. Sketch by
Theo. R. Davis in
HARPER'S WEEKLY, July 10, 1869.

The Icon on Display

No sooner had the State House bell been irreparably
cracked in early 1846 than city authorities
began talking about taking it down from the tower
and putting it on display where many more
people could see it. Philadelphians tend to consider
proposed innovations carefully, so it was not
until 1852 that the bell was removed from the tower
and placed in the Assembly Room of
Independence Hall, where Congress had met to
declare American independence.

As a contemporary description shows, the pedestal
upon which the bell was placed was anything but
conservative. It was:

*"...octagonal in shape with a double base. Upon the base are
placed, at the corners, eight fasces [a bundle of rods bound
around an axe with a projecting blade] surmounted by the
Liberty Cap and other emblems, and upon the fillets
which bind the reeds of these fasces, are tastefully arranged
the names of the Signers of the Declaration of Independence,
indicative of the effect of that act in binding the Union
together. Upon the fasces are shields -one containing the coat
of arms of the United States; a second, the arms of the State
of Pennsylvania; a third, the arms of the city of
Philadelphia;...The American flag is gracefully festooned
between the fasces, and binds them by its ample folds...The
bell is surmounted by a large gilt eagle."*

Appropriately, this pedestal was designed by
Frederick Graff. In 1776 it was Graff's grandfather,
Jacob, who rented two rooms to Thomas Jefferson.
There, in a small brick house at 7th and High
[now Market] Streets, Jefferson drafted the Declara-
tion of Independence.

Charles W. Alexander and M. Jules Jusserand, French Ambassador holding the Washington-Lafayette- Album Flag of the Revolution in front of the Liberty Bell. September 6, 1917. Photo by B. Wallace, Philadelphia.

1950s promotional photo.

Liberty Bell Sit-In, March 1965.

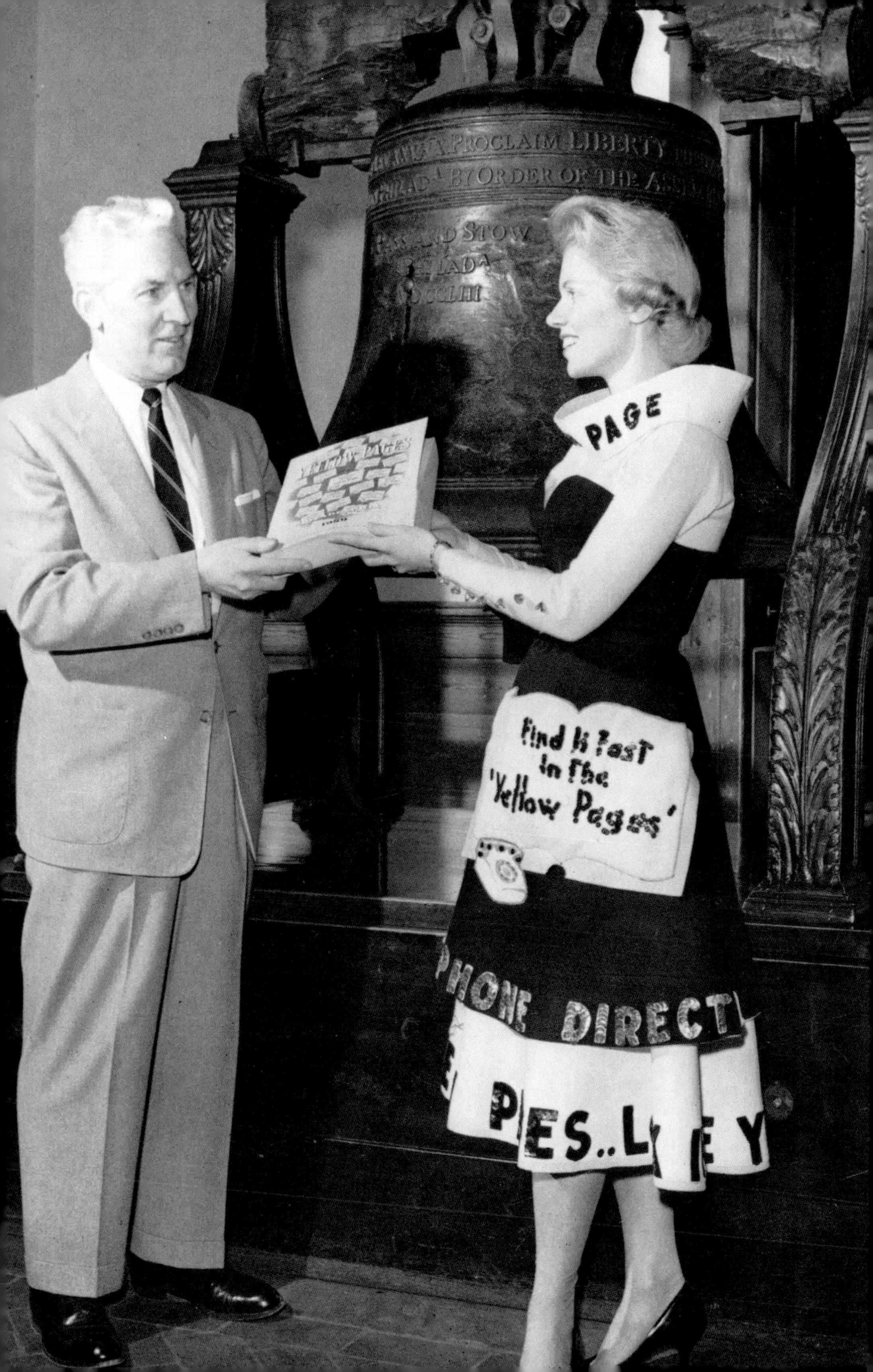
PROCLAIM LIBERTY
PAGE
Find It Fast
In the
'Yellow Pages'

The bell remained on display in the Assembly Room of Independence Hall throughout the Civil War. In 1873, the frame built for it in 1785 when it was rehung in the tower of Independence Hall, but by 1873 thought to be original, was brought down to the first floor and used to rehang the bell. Just after the centennial, in 1877, a more novel approach to displaying the bell was used. Removed from its yoke, the bell was suspended from the ceiling of the tower's first floor room using a chain of thirteen links.

Indicative of the bell's growing fame, in November 1884, the city of New Orleans asked Philadelphia to send the bell there for the World's Industrial and Cotton Centennial Exposition. The request noted that, *"Our ancestors fought and bled for the time enduring principles which that bell rang out on July 4, 1776, and, although the bell is the property of the City of Philadelphia, yet are we not co-inheritors of its glories?"* Apparently Philadelphia agreed because on January 23, 1885, the bell was loaded onto a special railroad car and sent to New Orleans.

A new chapter in the bell's evolution had begun. The
bell was about to become a very popular
traveling emissary of liberty and national unity.
After New Orleans, the bell visited Chicago
(1893 for the World's Columbian Exposition), Atlanta
(1895-96 for the Cotton States and International
Exposition), Charleston, S.C. (1902 for the Inter-State
and West Indian Exposition), Boston (1903 for
the 128th anniversary of the Battle of Bunker Hill),
St. Louis (1904 for the Louisiana Purchase
Exposition), and San Francisco (1915 for the Panama-
Pacific Exposition).

While the bell was in Chicago in 1893, what appeared
to be a new crack was discovered. Thereafter,
each proposed trip aroused increasing opposition from
Philadelphians. And, after the 1915 San Francisco
trip, all requests for the bell to travel were
denied. Since 1915 it has moved only three times, and
only within the city of Philadelphia. Twice
it paraded through Philadelphia during the Liberty
Loan drives of 1917 and 1918, and finally it
moved from Independence Hall to its new pavilion on
Independence Mall at midnight of January 1, 1976.

The Bells of Independence Hall

*In addition to the Liberty Bell,
five other bells have been
associated with Independence
Hall over the years. They are:*

🔔 *An August 19, 1854,*
PUBLIC LEDGER *report on
repairs being made to
Independence Hall stated that
"in the left (loft or attic) of
the building has been found a
bell, which is supposed to
have been...used in the steeple of
the old court house at Second
and Market Streets. It has the
inscription 'William
Weightman, 1682...recast by
T. J. Dyne, Jr. 1740.' "*

*This bell may have been
the one tradition says was hung
in a tree to call the early
Assemblies to their sessions. It
probably hung in the cupola
shown in Hamilton's perspective
of the proposed State House.
We have no other record of it,
and don't know where it is.*

🔔🔔 *The second Whitechapel
bell. This bell was hung in
the cupola of the State House for
the clock to strike on. When
a new clock was included in the
1828 steeple, the old clock and
bell were given to St. Augustine's
Roman Catholic Church
at Fourth and New Streets.
The church was burned by a
mob in 1844, and the
bell partly melted. The remains
were recast. That bell is
at Villanova University.*

🔔🔔🔔 *On February 8, 1821,
Philadelphia City Councils
resolved to pay Councilman
William Meredith $484.95
"to be applied in payment of the
Cost of the New State House
clock Bell, and of the expense of
putting the same up etc."
We assume that it replaced the
second Whitechapel bell in
the cupola, and that it was this
1821 bell that was sold to John
Wilbank in 1828.*

🔔🔔🔔🔔 *In 1828,
John Wilbank cast a 4,000
pound bell for the new
steeple. His first attempt did
not satisfy Philadelphians,
but a second effort was raised
to the steeple late in that year.
In 1876, this bell, and the 1828
steeple clock, were moved to
the Germantown Town Hall,
where they remain.*

🔔🔔🔔🔔🔔 *In 1876,
a wealthy and eccentric
Philadelphian, Henry Seybert,
presented the city with a
new steeple clock and bell. The
13,000 pound bell was cast
by the Meneely and Kimberly
foundry in Troy, New York.
The bell was in place to
ring on the one hundredth
anniversary of American independence, but the city didn't
like its sound. As did Pass and
Stow and John Wilbank,
Meneely had to cast a second bell
(Philadelphians are picky
about their bells). This bell is the
one which now booms
forth from Independence Hall
each hour.*

Bell "tapped" for
transcontinental phone service.
February 11, 1915.

However, while the bell itself no longer traveled,
its sound did. With the advent of electronic
amplification, it became possible to tap the bell with
a mallet, and transmit the resulting sound. This
was done for the first time on February 11, 1915,
when the bell was struck three times to initiate
transcontinental telephone service. The process has
been repeated many times, most notably on the
225th anniversary of Benjamin Franklin's birth (January 1931), on the 200th anniversary of Washington's
birth (February 1932), on D-Day (June 6, 1944), and
on VE and VJ Days (May 8 and August 14, 1945).

The Liberty Bell on tour.

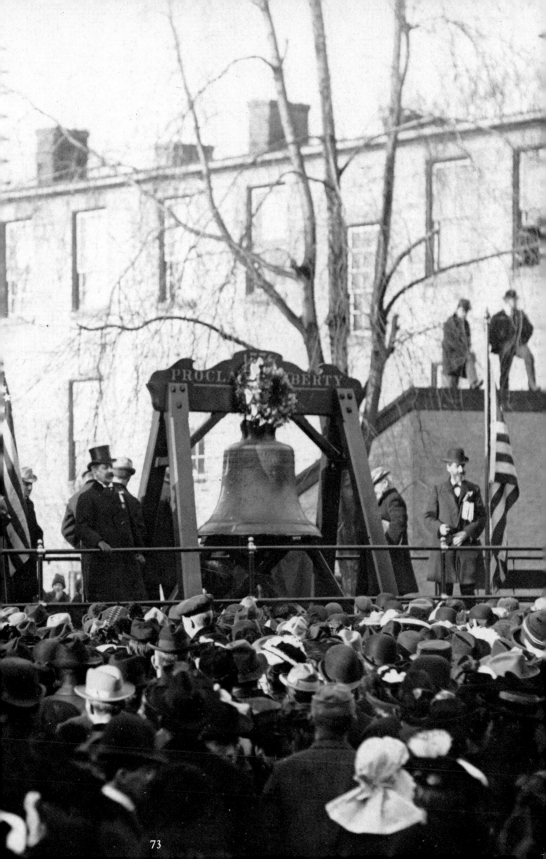

Paying homage to the bell,
both the real bell and a replica.

Almost home.
The bell's last trip, 1915.

Conclusion

Looking back, the hold that a cracked and useless bell has come to have on the American people is amazing. This hold is perhaps best shown by popular reaction during its several trips. Every effort was made to route it so as many people as possible could see it. Astounding crowds turned out all along its routes. In Chicago; Baltimore; Cleveland; St. Louis; and Los Angeles as well as in Wabasha, Minnesota; Marengo, Iowa; Doswell, Virginia; and Bowie, Arizona, thousands paid homage to what the bell had come to symbolize. On its very first trip, no less a personage than former United States Senator, United States Secretary of War, and Confederate States of America President Jefferson Davis traveled to Biloxi, Mississippi to see the bell. Since it represented traditional freedoms in which all Americans believed, Davis said, the bell's trip would help heal the Nation's wounds.

Now, over a century later, the bell's healing powers remain undiminished, perhaps even enhanced by the passage of time. In the 20th century, the bell's message has transcended national boundaries, attracting visitors from around the world. Not only does each U.S. state display a replica of the bell, but there are also copies in Japan and Israel. Once again, the bell seems to be entering another phase in its continuing evolution. Slowly the transformation proceeds with the next chapter in the history of the bell yet to be written.

This book was designed by
Burns, Connacher, & Waldron New York, NY.
Cover and memorabilia
photography was done by Thomas Landon Davies,
National Park Service